The How To Be British Collection Two

Martyn Ford

Peter Legon

***The* How To Be British Collection Two**
Published by Lee Gone Publications, 11 Kenya Court, Windlesham Gardens,
Brighton, East Sussex, GB BN1 3AU.

First published 2005.

© Martyn Ford, Peter Legon 2005. All rights reserved.

Artwork by Martyn Ford.

ISBN 0 - 9522870 - 4 - 8

Printed and bound in Britain by Judges of Hastings.

1 *Entry Test*

Test your eligibility for citizenship with this short quiz on aspects of British life and culture. Choose **a**, **b** or **c**.

1   British food is
    a. the best in the world
    b. the best in the U.K.
    c. best avoided

2   To become British, you need
    a. Union Jack underpants
    b. your own teapot
    c. more than fifteen piercings

3   The Battle of Hastings (1066) was won by
    a. Henry IV (Part One)
    b. Eastbourne
    c. An illegal immigrant

4   'Spotted Dick' is
    a. an illness
    b. a new reality TV game show
    c. a British teenage boy

5   The currency in Britain is called
    a. the punt
    b. the pint
    c. the pee

6   Britain is
    a. in Europe
    b. outside Europe
    c. Europe

for Andrew Kenny

Brain of Britain

language learning facility
(not visible to naked eye)

Royal Family
cognition centre

nostalgia
segment

mistrust of Europe
ventricle

national pride gland
(likely to become inflamed
during World Cup)

bottled-up
anger

tea

beer

custard
(for Scotland, see 'porridge')

pastry

sea

traditional
breakfast

repository of useless
facts for pub quiz nights

Isle of Wight

love of countryside

BACKBONE!

outside world

hat

rain

unused
section

head

hatband

brim

2 *Great Britons*

To be a Great Briton it is not enough to do something original and marvellous; it is essential that ordinary Britons can understand it. Charles Darwin, for example, is Great because he pointed out that we are close relatives of more primitive life forms lower down the evolutionary chain - a truth evident to anyone who finds an old sofa or TV set dumped in their front garden. Robin Hood is Great because he brought tourism to Nottingham and Florence Nightingale because of her lamp.

A minimum qualification for greatness is to have a distinguishing characteristic that enables ordinary people to pick you out from the crowd: an unusual hat, a two-fingered salute, round glasses or only one arm.

In no way should foreigners feel debarred from seeking the status of Great Briton. It is a time-honoured custom here for high-achievers from overseas to be redesignated as British, as long as they agree not to mention their origins, and to give all the credit for their triumphs to their adoptive country.

Expressions to learn
He shaped our island history and, indeed, the destiny of all mankind.

Avoid saying
What's so great about introducing tobacco and potatoes to Britain?

3 *You Are Here*

But where exactly? And what is the address? Many foreign visitors are understandably confused. *Britain* is a *nation* and the people who live here are *British nationals* or *Britons* (apart from those who are visiting or hiding here). This doesn't include *Ireland*, which is really called *Eire*, and was part of Britain once but isn't now, except that is for *Northern Ireland (Ulster)*, where the people are *Irish*, of course (and not *English*), but are also part of the *United Kingdom* (although some object to this), which consists of *England*, *Scotland* and *Wales*, as well as *Ulster*, which have separate *parliaments* (except Wales, which has an *assembly* and Ulster which has *power sharing*), but not the *Isle of Man*, which is neither part of Britain nor the United Kingdom, although its residents are classified as 'Manx British', nor the *Channel Islands*, which are *dependencies of the British crown*, though all of the aforementioned are part of the *British Isles* (see *Great Britain*). Any questions?

Expressions to learn
I'm an ethnic Chinese Welshman with British nationality living in Scotland.
Are you a Kentish man or a man of Kent?

Avoid saying
So how does the European Union affect this?
Say what you like, it's all the same country.

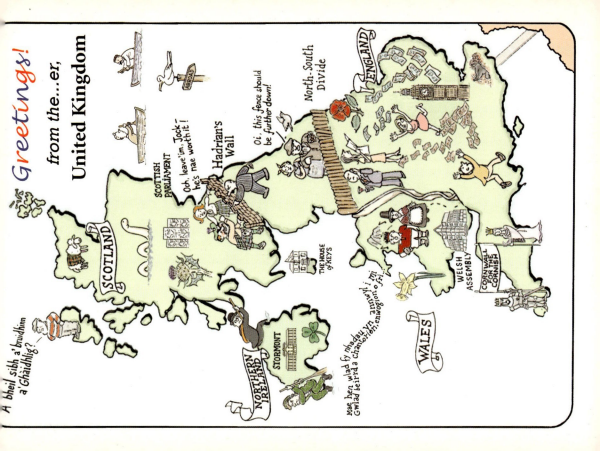

4 *For England and St. George*

On April 23rd every year, patriotic English people hang the flag of St. George from their houses, paint their faces red and white, and think of England ... or, at least, *try* to. For the sad fact is that while the Scots, the Welsh and the Irish are only too happy to explain at length who *they* are, the English are rather at a loss. This was not always so, of course: brides in Victorian times were advised to 'close your eyes and think of England' on their wedding night. This was to remind them that, however unpleasant it might be, they were doing their duty to their country (an idea that many older readers will agree has rather fallen out of fashion lately). So what reassuring images of England and its great history did those innocent brides summon up to reassure or anaesthetise? The waves breaking on Dover Beach? James Watt's mighty steam engine? Or just a steaming hot dish of toad in the hole? Sadly, we shall never know.

Expressions to learn
Oh, to be in England, now that April's there!

Avoid saying
Of course, St. George came from the Middle East, you know.

5 *O'er the Border and Awa'*

It is sometimes said that the Scots are *dour* because of their rugged landscape and harsh weather, and the roughness of their woollens against the skin. *Foreign* visitors, however, will find them friendly and hospitable. For a taste of the 'real' Scotland, take the High Road (or the Low Road) to Edinburgh to watch the soldiers at the castle displaying their military tattoos (mostly scenes of victory over the 'auld enemy').

Next it's on to the Highlands where activities abound. Learn to toss the caber (also known as the Highland Fling), attend a bagpipe workshop, dance a ceilidh or two, then as the midnight sun slowly sets, hire a rowing boat and relive the romantic journey of Bonnie Prince Charlie in 1746 as he escaped over the sea to Skye disguised as a haggis. An official guide will lead you miles over burns, banks and braes to his lonely crofter's cottage where, by a roaring peat fire, you can nibble your way through a box of shortbread and sample your host's entire collection of 120 single malts.

Expressions to learn
A plate of neeps and tatties and an Auld Reekie chaser, please.

Avoid saying
Can you repeat that, Jock, but this time in English?

..and coming up on our right, one of the most magnificent views in the whole of the Highlands — the stark grandeur of the Gilliemuir Mountains and Glen Lairg where the Nairns were massacred by the McKeiths, and the romantic ruins of Dunleekie Castle, reflected in the shimmering expanse of Loch .... oh, dear, the mists's come down again! Never mind, f you'd like to turn to the screen at the front of the bus, you can see the same scene on video, filmed last year, when....

6 *Double Vision*

The Welsh are blessed with two tongues, a great advantage for a country of politicians and place names beginning with 'Ll'. It also gives them the edge when it comes to singing, and there's plenty to sing about: a proud industrial heritage, their own prince, sporting triumphs, a popular cheesy snack. Most of all, however, the Welsh are renowned for their sobriety, as is exemplified by the following story:

Whilst on a missionary expedition to the jungles of Borneo, a Welshman became separated from the rest of his party. Nineteen years later, he was discovered by two explorers. Proudly, the man took them on a guided tour of his settlement. They were struck, in particular, by two identical timber buildings he had constructed at opposite ends of the clearing. The Welshman explained that these were chapels. The explorers knew the Welsh to be a pious people, but were puzzled nonetheless. "Why *two* chapels?" they asked. "Ah, well, you see," replied the man, "this one here is the chapel I go to, and that one over there is the chapel I *don't go to*."

Expressions to learn
Our holiday cottage lies between Blaenau-Ffestiniog and Penrhyndeudraeth.

Avoid saying
Do you think they're talking about us?

7 *Making Tracks*

It is all too common these days to hear rail travellers grumbling into their mobiles about delays, cancellations and failed trains. But such things are really minor inconveniences when compared to the huge improvements made in the provision of continental-style coffee and pastries on station forecourts, not to mention the gaily-coloured uniforms of the many private rail companies whose trains come and go (or remain) at the platforms.

We apologise for the late running of this train, which is due to the length of the journey.
All of us at some time have sat on a train, wondering why it's not moving or the lights have suddenly gone out. But it's all too easy to criticise and to forget that the railways have had to deal with years of under-investment. Getting from A to B is not the straightforward business it used to be. At least we can now listen to a cheerful recorded announcement informing us of the driver's name, or that the buffet has just closed. We should stop grumbling, sit back and enjoy the ride. Or, rather, the wait.

Expressions to learn
Take your time, driver, we're not in a hurry.

Avoid saying
I could have walked there by now.

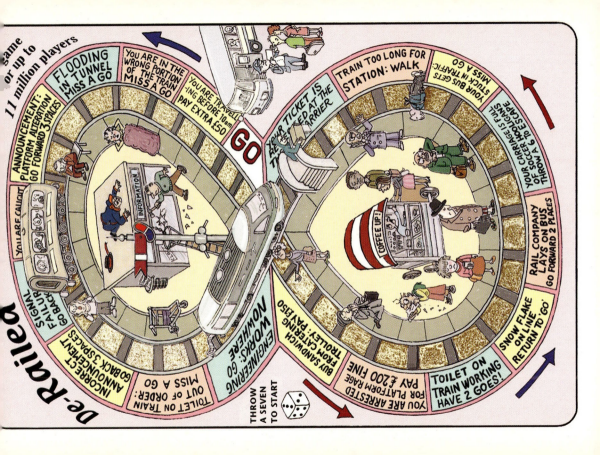

8 *Cricket*

Cricket is not merely a sport, but part of *the English soul*, and visitors should treat it with the quiet respect accorded to the rites of an unfamiliar religion.

Although the general aim of the *batting* side is to score runs and the *bowling* side to take *wickets*, the main priority for all is to enjoy a pleasant afternoon in the fresh air and work up an appetite for tea. It should be treated not so much as a contest, but as a shared activity, like building a bonfire or putting up a tent (activities also likely to be interrupted by rain).

Cricket is a common topic of earnest conversation in pubs and places of work, particularly in the summer. Even if you never play or watch a match it is recommended that you familiarize yourself with some basic cricketing terms in order not to be socially and culturally disadvantaged. For example, *Perkins is out - caught in the slips off the bowling of Glover for 9*. Or, *What a splendid cover drive by Wilkins!*

Expressions to learn
He can't complain; he's had a good innings.

Avoid saying
I'm bored. Can we go home?

...and the winning run is the one to Mrs. Thorogood's Victoria sponge!

9 *The Full English*

Fried egg, streaky bacon, sausage, grilled tomato, mushrooms, baked beans, black pudding, a fried slice, not to mention the obligatory starters and accompaniments: grapefruit segments, stewed prunes, cereals, porridge, numerous rounds of toast, butter and marmalade, and, of course, unlimited cups of tea. With a head start like that no wonder the British built an Empire that girdled the earth, while their unlucky competitors struggled out into the world with only a bowl of milky coffee and a tiny bun to line their stomachs.

Sadly, in these decadent days, it is left to a determined few to start the day with the time-honoured 'fry-up'. The rest run from bed to bathroom to front door pausing only to grab a 'breakfast bar' or some equally degenerate snack substitute.

Happily though 'the full English' survives in transport cafés and B&Bs throughout the land and the emergence of the popular 'all-day breakfast' clearly demonstrates that the time is ripe for the British once more to fulfil their potential on the world's stage.

Expressions to use
A number three 'gutbuster', please, with two extra rashers and double mushrooms.

Avoid saying
I'll just have a brioche and a latté, please.

There's only one thing to do after a

Full English Breakfast...

go back to bed and sleep it off till lunchtime !

10 *Land of Hope and Gravy*

The close-knit British family keeps tradition alive in the cherished ritual of sitting down together to Sunday lunch. At the heart of this ritual is the *Sunday joint*, roasted in its juices with potatoes and parsnips, and accompanied by steaming heaps of cabbage, carrots, peas and sprouts, plus, if beef is on the menu, *Yorkshire pudding*. This whole collation is then drenched with rich brown *gravy* - one of the world's greatest, though still alas unsung, sauces.

As lunch is prepared, the family gather round the wireless and listen to a programme of record requests played for brave members of the British Armed Forces serving in far flung corners of the Empire, who are constrained to live in little huts with names like 'BFPO 17'. Then Mother calls everyone to the table, Father carves the roast, and it's "Dig in!"

After a brief interval to debate the top political and religious issues of the day, a steaming suet pudding is served, speckled with sultanas, over which is poured hot yellow *custard* - another sadly under-rated British sauce.

Expressions to learn
More crackling, Grandma?

Avoid saying
Can I have mine in a sesame seed bun with cucumber relish?

11 *Making a Meal of It*

The foreign visitor invited to a British home for a meal should be aware of the precise terminology we use to describe what we eat and when we eat it. This is to avoid the embarrassment of arriving five hours early (or late), too hungry or not hungry enough.

Lunch: almost certainly in the middle of the day. May consist of anything from sandwiches to a three-course meal.
Luncheon: you will need to use a serviette.
Dinner: in the South of England around 7 or 8pm, but north of The Wash probably a hot meal in the middle of the day.
Tea: could be sandwiches, tea and cake at 4pm, or up North a hot meal around 5.30.
High tea: a larger meal than tea, probably involving pork pie and sliced beetroot.
Supper: used by metropolitan sophisticates to mean dinner (braised ptarmigan and halloumi patties with a blueberry coulis, etc.) eaten fairly late in the evening; to humbler folk, a bedtime snack such as cheese biscuits with a hot milky drink.

Expressions to learn
A spot of lunch; a turkey dinner; a fish supper; a slap-up meal.

Avoid saying
I expected something a bit more substantial than this.

Breakfast

Brunch

Elevenses

Lunch (dinner)

Tea

High tea (dinner)

Dinner (supper)

Supper

12 *Cap and Gown*

Britain has some of the oldest and most prestigious universities in the world. Young people who want the best continue to favour these ancient seats of learning, to sit and study at the very same ink-stained benches where sat the illustrious historians, poets, scientists and philosophers who shaped our modern world. In former times, places in higher education were accessible only to the privileged classes, and entrance exams discriminated on the basis of academic ability. Now, happily, all this has changed.

Thanks to new 'equal opportunities' exams, almost any young person who's got the money can enjoy the benefits of superb resources and tuition. Once, undergraduates were compelled to study abstruse subjects like Mathematics, Geography and Literature, but now courses such as Leisure Marketing, Tennis Court Management, Hip Hop Studies and Money Laundering prepare them for real life and the world of work.

Expressions to learn
I'm doing a GNVQ in ICT at a CHE that used to be a CAT.
Another tequila slammer, anyone?

Avoid saying
Are you sure you haven't downloaded this dissertation?
Everywhere calls itself a 'university' these days.

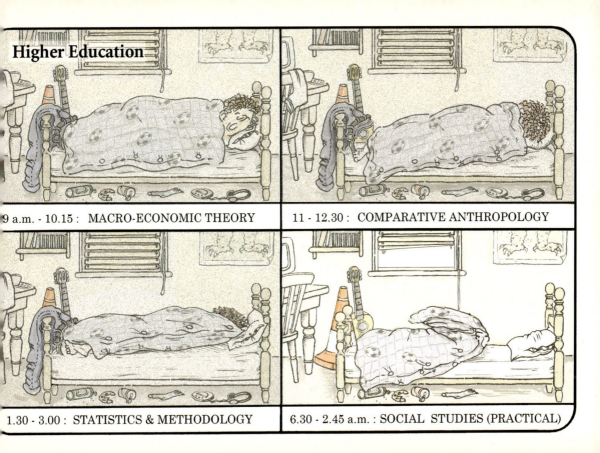

13 *Grammar Rules, OK?*

As the name suggests, the English language originated in *England*, and while we are content, even proud, to lend it out to others for use as an international language, we do so on the understanding that it is really ours. We British should be the first to be consulted over controversial questions of grammar and usage. If people in other lands want to say 'different *to*' instead of 'different *from*' they should at least ask us first.

We have toiled for centuries to cultivate a vital distinction between the Present Perfect and Past Simple Tenses:
"**I've** already **had** an iced bun, thanks. I **had** the one with the pink icing."
Yet in some countries it is possible to hear the following exchange:
"Do you want an iced bun?" "Why, Mom, I **already had** one."
The neglect of such distinctions can cause serious ambiguity, and in extreme cases lead to mid-air collisions or accidental invasions of sovereign territory.

Expressions to learn
Do please point out my mistakes - I'm trying to make *fewer* of them.

Avoid saying
It's tedious to always go on about split infinitives.

Mrs Hoover, you are always saying, "I'm just going to 'lay down' for five minutes" but here it says that the correct form of the intransitive verb is 'to lie' and that the verb 'to lay' must take a direct object, as in the expression 'She laid the table...'

14 *The Ins and Outs of It*

Think back to the last time you had cornflakes for breakfast. Did you eat the cornflakes dry? Probably not. There was milk, wasn't there? Now think back carefully: where exactly was the milk? Was it *on* the cornflakes, *in* the cornflakes, *by* the cornflakes, *beside* the cornflakes, *beneath* the cornflakes or *betwixt* the cornflakes? It could have been any of those, and the way in which you ate your breakfast would have been materially affected by which of them it was.

It is the great strength of English that it has the means to express so many exciting relationships between objects in the physical world. But it doesn't end there...

One or more of these versatile little words can attach themselves to the end of a 'normal' verb to create phrasal verbs (*shape up, chicken out, string along, groove on down to,* etc.), expressions so idiomatic that even the most advanced foreign learners are baffled, a state of affairs that native speakers have been known to use to their advantage.

Expressions to learn
Do you expect this rain to peter out by dusk?

Avoid saying
Anything ending in 'off'.

up

down

on

next to

away

off

out

back

15 *A Word of Advice*

As everyone knows, the right word at the right moment can make all the difference to a successful social encounter. Fortunately, there is one word in particular that will endear the visitor to Brits of all ranks and conditions. What is this most estimable of exclamations, this acme of adjectives? Why, it is *lovely,* of course!

It makes no difference whether you are being invited to admire the speaker's new hair-do, flowering shrubs, sitting-room curtains or grandchildren: they will all, inevitably, be *lovely*. It is not enough that you both *know* everything is lovely, it must be stated, emphatically, with a rising intonation on the first syllable.

A word of warning: despite the versatility of this little word, it is important to observe the speaker's facial expression and tone of voice to determine her attitude to the news she is imparting. This is to avoid pragmatic errors such as the following:

> HOSTESS: And this is a photo of my late husband, who was gored by a warthog on our honeymoon in Bongandanga.
> VISITOR: Oh, lovely!

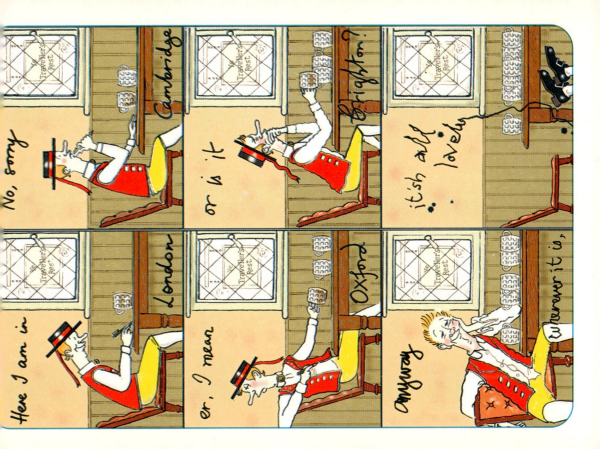

16 *Essential Kings and Queens*

Boudicca (1st century A.D.) Warrior queen and first woman driver (see *Woad Rage*). Resisted Roman attempts to introduce hot baths, straight roads and sandals with socks.

Arthur (6th century A.D.) United Britain with magical sword of truth and justice. Pledged to return one day but currently lost in the mists of time.

Alfred the Great (871-899) Proved that the Danes were resistible and that Anglo-Saxon men were better at slaying than home baking.

William the Conqueror (1066-1087) Norman king who unfairly defeated the Anglo-Saxons in 1066 with the appalling consequence that everyone had to learn a foreign language.

Henry V (1413-1422) Got revenge for 1066 by defeating foppish French aristocrats at the Battle of Agincourt. Demonstrated that English soldiers fight best when outnumbered by at least ten to one.

Henry VIII (1509-1547) Promoted family values and boosted the popularity of marriage by taking six wives in succession to ensure the Succession.

Elizabeth I (1558-1603) Singed the beard of the King of Spain after he improperly proposed to her, then defeated his Armada, proving that Britannia Rules the Waves.

Charles I (1625-1649) Made himself unpopular by behaving in a cavalier fashion. Insisted he was divine, so Parliament cut off his head to show that he wasn't.

Victoria (1837-1901) Taught us that if you were Top Nation you had to set a good example to other, subject nations by dressing soberly and not laughing at vulgar jokes.

17 *Peers of Our Realm*

In Britain, it is essential to know who is above you socially (and if you are a foreign visitor that will be everyone, more or less). Owing to wars and revolutions, or simple carelessness, many European nations have lost these important distinctions between persons of quality and the rest of us. Happily, we British have preserved them in the form of the *peerage* - an ancient system of classification of the ranks or degrees of nobility.

Sadly, even some Brits are no longer entirely sure of the difference between a *belted earl* and a *baronet* or how they should address a duke (the answer is 'Your Grace'). This uncertainty can result in a loss of respect for the social order and a mistaken assumption that everyone is equal.

To answer one frequently asked question: you get to be an earl because your father was an earl, whereas you are made a knight by the Queen for doing something outstanding for the nation, e.g. appearing in the tabloid newspapers for more than twenty-three weeks in succession.

Expressions to learn
I've seen your coat of arms everywhere!
I am indeed most obliged to you, Your Grace.

Avoid saying
Yes, but what does a duke actually *do*?
What a lot of outdated nonsense!

Duke

Duchess

Marquess

Countess

Earl

Viscount

Baron

Lords Spiritual

Knight

Esquire

Gentleman

Commoner

18 *Mind Your Own Business*

The peace and quiet of an anonymous-looking suburban street is suddenly shattered by the dramatic arrest of one of the residents for some horrible crime. In a break with convention, neighbours come out of their houses and talk to one another. And when the camera crews and reporters arrive, they always say the same thing: "I can't believe it - he seemed such a nice chap. His front hedge was always neatly trimmed, and *he always kept himself to himself*." A respect for privacy is one of the most esteemed social virtues in Britain, and those who offend against it are branded 'nosey Parkers'.

Householders in foreign lands may sit outside their front doors, shelling peas and chatting to the world at large, or else hang from their balconies calling down to passers-by in the street. Such behaviour makes the British deeply uneasy. The semi-detached suburban house has a garden back and front, but it is an unwritten rule never to sit in the *front* garden. That would appear to invite casual conversation with every passing Tom, Dick or Harry, and who knows *where* that might end!

Expressions to learn
We've got delightful people next door - you wouldn't know they were there.

Avoid saying
Drop in any time you like.

19 *It's Only a Scratch*

However bad things get the True Brit knows that it doesn't do to make a fuss. One of the most stinging reproofs in English is "Oh, don't be so *dramatic*!" The British way of dealing with disaster is to refuse to take it too seriously, to dismiss it with a droll joke or euphemism. So if a huge lump of ice falls from a plane and crashes through the roof of your house, then remember that the proper response is a shrugged, "Oh well. Can't be helped. I was going to replace those chair covers anyway."

Suppose, in some far-off future time, we are told that an asteroid fifty miles wide is hurtling unstoppably towards us, and that whatever is left of Earth after the shattering impact will go spinning off into deep, dark interstellar space: you can be certain that somewhere amidst the global lamentations, if you listen very hard, you will hear a British voice saying quietly, in level tones, "Never mind. Worse things happen at sea!"

Expressions to learn
It wasn't exactly a bed of roses, but we managed.

Avoid saying
Come on - get it off your chest.

Great British Virtues

No. 47 *Making the Best of Things*

Look on the bright side: at least it's stopped raining ...and some of these sandwiches are still dry!

20 *One's Own Trumpet*

As far as the True Brit is concerned, it is very bad form to crow about one's successes. The British take modesty a step further into actual self-disparagement. This is simply a question of good manners. In order not to be written off as a 'big-head', you must learn to play down your accomplishments.

In other countries if you rise to the pinnacle of your profession you will tell your friends: "They wanted the most talented and dynamic person they could get, so they hired me." This would be very bad form in Britain, where you should say: "Oh I just happened to be in the right place at the right time. Luckily, they've never found me out!"

The whole point of social life here is not to antagonize others, not to *get up people's noses*. So don't go on about the size of your nest-egg or how gifted your children are; instead, pull a face and tell us how your recent holiday was 'an absolute nightmare!' You'll soon be drawing on an inexhaustible fund of sympathy and commiseration.

Expressions to learn
Well, I *do* have a Rolls Royce, but it's only a small one.

Avoid saying
Come into the den and I'll show you my golfing trophies.

WRONG

RIGHT

21 *Saturday Night*

It's Saturday night and a group of upright young lads in clean white shirts, suits and ties are on their way to their favourite city dance hall. For the unattached amongst them this is the one chance in the week to meet and get to know a young lady.

But, oh dear, the ladies are all dancing in groups - how on earth does a fellow get an introduction? The braver ones go right up and ask for the pleasure of the next dance; the shy ones just stand in the shadows and wistfully sip their half pint of shandy. At 5 past 11 the band finishes with a slow, smoochy song and everyone heads for the exit and the last bus home.

The weekend revels are nearly over: there may be time for a hasty bag of fish and chips on the walk home from the bus stop, but by now everyone's tired and eager for bed. It's all been *such* fun, but tomorrow is Sunday, and they mustn't be late for church.

Expressions to learn
Would you care for another sparkling apple juice?
It's nice to see young people enjoying themselves.

Avoid saying
It's like a battlefield out there.
Are you looking at me, mate?

22 *The Thought That Counts*

The British love greetings cards. If you wish to be popular, you should send these to your British friends on every possible occasion. For example:
Good Luck in your New Trousers!
Sorry to hear about your Hamster.
Congratulations on your Vasectomy.

Of course, we also love giving and receiving presents. There is some important etiquette involved in this, which the foreigner would do well to observe.

     VISITOR: Here, I bought this for you.
     BRITISH PERSON: For me? But...
     VIS: It's only a little something.
     BRIT: Oh, you shouldn't go spending your money on me!
     VIS: Really, it's nothing. I've kept the receipt in case you want to change it.
     BRIT: Change it? Oh no, it's *perfect!*
     VIS: I had no idea what to get you.
     BRIT: But it's *wonderful!*
     VIS: Well, it was luck, really... I saw it and thought of you.
     BRIT: It's absolutely brilliant. Thank you *so* much.
     VIS: Not at all. I'm glad you like it.
     BRIT: I *will* take the receipt, though, if you've still got it. Just in case.
     VIS: Of course! Here you are.

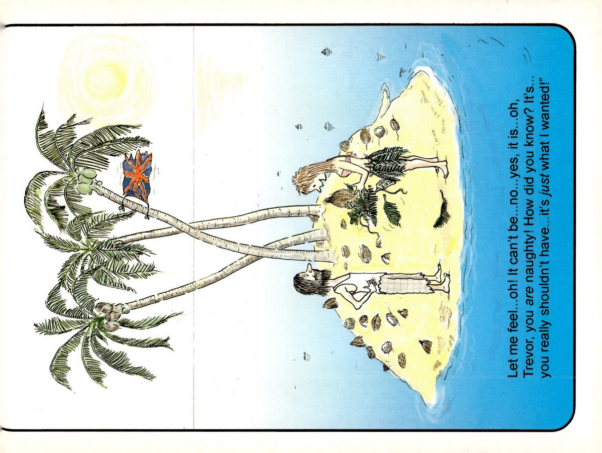

"Let me feel...oh! It can't be...no...yes, it is...oh, Trevor, you are naughty! How did you know? It's... you really shouldn't have...it's *just* what I wanted!"

23 *May Day*

On 1st May take a break from international socialism and head for the nearest English village. Wait outside the pub until the *squire* invites you to take part in traditional *Morris* dancing on the green. The *sides* are usually male and drawn from a cross-section of lawyers and social science lecturers. You will be supplied with the appropriate dress of bowler hat, white shirt, knee-length breeches and socks (with bells attached). You will need your own clean white handkerchief to wave at the other dancers and a stout stick or *staff* for when you clash with them. The May Day celebrations originate in pre-Christian fertility rituals; however, this should not be seen as a licence to test the virtue of the village maidens, gathered for the 'Queen of the May' competition. Leg-lifting should be confined to the dance itself, and proof of manly prowess to the consumption of pints of *real ale*. It is permitted, however, to sing one or two earthy folk songs, as long as they were collected from the local blacksmith over 100 years ago by a scholarly clergyman eager to preserve our oral heritage.

Expressions to learn
Rifle, rifle, fol - di-diddle i-dol.

Avoid saying
How many locals can afford to live in this village now? Tell me that!

Bad news, Professor. I'm afraid some _real_ folk have just arrived!

24 *Bonfire Night*

One traditional celebration found only in England is Bonfire Night, on November 5th, the anniversary of the Gunpowder Plot. This was an attempt, led by Guy Fawkes, to blow up King and Parliament. Many foreign visitors tactlessly assume we are celebrating the *attempt* itself, whereas of course we are rejoicing at its *failure*.

The *traditional* Bonfire Night should be spent with family and friends in the back garden, standing around a bonfire of damp twigs, mattresses, old tyres, etc., on top of which sits an effigy of the *guy* (Fawkes) in Gran's old cardigan. Trembling dogs and cats are shut into the sitting room; women and children stand safely back, and the oldest male of the household flits back and forth in the darkness with a torch and a small box of assorted fireworks, lighting the blue touchpaper of rockets, roman candles and catherine wheels. Children practise writing their names in the air with sparklers; potatoes and chestnuts are tossed into the embers of the fire to roast; and the whole evening ends when a spark accidentally sets light to next door's trellis.

Expressions to learn
Woooooooooh! Aaaaaaaaaaaaaah! Did you see that one?
That last rocket went straight through the Hudsons' greenhouse!

Avoid saying
Round our way there are bangs every night for three weeks.
Are you sure this doesn't foment religious intolerance?

That's just typical of the Larkins — every November 5th they have to go one better than us!

25 *Next Year It's Weston-Super-Mare*

Perhaps because of the unpredictability of their own summers, the British are drawn to hotter, drier climates where they will be able to say "Lovely day today, isn't it?" *every single day*. But their very enthusiasm is their undoing. They go out for a noon-day stroll, hatless and topless, drink a little of the local wine in order to be friendly, then wake up on the beach four hours later looking like overturned pillar boxes. Moreover, the rough and tumble of life abroad - squashed up against strangers on crowded buses, pestered to buy rugs and seashells, having to deal with 'gippy tummy', lost wallets or offended locals and all in a strange language - quickly proves too much for them.

The one positive aspect of the exercise is the sudden realisation of just how much they miss home - their own bed, orderly queues, pork scratchings, refreshing drizzle and, above all, *everything written in English!*

Expressions to learn
Toasted teacakes and a pot of tea for two, please.
Val - these good people live just off Darley Drive!

Avoid saying
When in Rome do as the Romans do.
Travel broadens the mind.

26 *Seaside Holidays*

It's mid-August and all along the esplanade the beach huts have thrown open their freshly-painted doors to the world. The beach itself - mile after mile of striped deckchairs and flapping wind-breaks - is thronged with skimpily-dressed visitors from industrial cities and provincial backwaters. Young men stripped to the waist show off their tattoos; girls with big legs and burnt shoulders carry huge pink teddy bears won at the rifle range; families with grizzling children queue for *99s* and paper cones of chips; silver-haired seniors, with several pints of tea in them, spill out of the Bingo Hall wondering where their coach has gone. And in the evening everyone's out again, strolling along the promenade to marvel at the illuminations, on their way to another sell-out show featuring some of the great TV stars of yesteryear.

There's nothing to beat a British seaside holiday. Filey, Skegness, Morecambe, Bognor Regis - such places virtually invented leisure. Bodrum, Miami, Alicante: they do their best but, let's face it, they are not Bexhill-on-Sea and they never will be.

Expressions to learn
I've been coming here for sixty years, man and boy.

Avoid saying
We could have had two weeks in the Crimea with what we've spent this weekend!

Ah, you can't beat a good old-fashioned British seaside holiday — no worries about harmful ultra-violet rays for us!

27 *London*

No tour of Britain is complete without a visit to London. Take a hackney carriage to Trafalgar Square, where you can feed the lions, pose for a photo with a friendly British 'bobby' and gasp in astonishment at Nelson's enormous column. Walk to Buckingham Palace in time to watch the sovereign emerge in her golden state coach; then head for Covent Garden to enjoy the cockney accents of burly barrow boys and pretty flower girls selling posies outside the Royal Opera House.

In the evening, travel east and drop into one of the many pubs along the Old Kent Road frequented by Pearly Kings and Queens, who will teach you to do the Hokey Kokey or the Lambeth Walk. After a pint of mild and a plate of jellied eels, make your way back to Westminster. Take up a position between the Abbey and Parliament. Put your hand over your wallet, close your eyes, and as Big Ben begins to chime, you will surely say to yourself: *I've had the time of my life!*

Expressions to learn
You put your left leg in, your left leg out…

Avoid saying
Are you sure you're taking me the most direct route, cabbie?

28 *Pounds Lighter*

In the bad old days, the health of the nation was something of an embarrassment. Jokes abounded about couch potatoes swilling lager and guzzling sausages, unable to get up and change the TV channel without a mechanical hoist. Happily, things are now very different. Due to enlightened government initiatives in areas such as fresh greens, fun runs, smoke-free swimming pools and low-alcohol puddings, the general population is looking fitter and leaner than ever.

Every January thousands of Brits join health and fitness clubs to row, lift, run and pedal their way to peak physical condition - or at least until it gets boring, or the special discount trial membership expires. Then the penny drops. What the body needs after all is pampering, not punishing. Aromatherapy, shiatsu, reiki, Indian head massage: the clinic of complementary medicine offers a welcome alternative to all that gasping and sweating. It even includes a one-to-one session with the life coach, who confirms what the patient already suspected: that the new investment is *just what the doctor ordered* - except he *didn't* order it because it's not on the National Health … yet.

Expressions to learn
Can you squeeze me in for an aqua detox between my reflexology and kinesiology?

Avoid saying
I'm not having needles stuck in me, and that's final.

29 *Digging for Victory*

To the True Brit a garden is not a place in which to loll on a sun-lounger reading the newspapers - it is a call to arms, a huge and open-ended responsibility, like bringing up children. While other Europeans may be content to water their window boxes, he (or just as often *she*) is out in the open, exposed to the rigours of the native climate, hacking at thistles, tying back the cotoneaster, or digging up a particularly tenacious lavatera.

What is it that drives him on? Is it really a love of flowers and growing things? Not entirely. Somewhere deep inside him there is an ancestral memory of times when wars and shortages meant growing your own. That's why he is so proud of those ungainly cucumbers, those leathery cabbages and oversized marrows.

And there are other rewards, perhaps, of a more reflective kind: burning leaves on a summer's evening, forking the potato peelings into the compost heap, or simply taking refuge in the sanctuary of his shed.

Expressions to learn
I like my husband where I can see him.

Avoid saying
I don't know why you bother - they'll only get eaten by the slugs.

30 *Do It Ourselves*

In other parts of the world builders build, plumbers plumb, and decorators do the decorating; in Britain such a dependence on mere professionals would be a source of shame. Here, to be called 'handy' is the highest possible praise.

Our Brit takes a pride in his chipping, chiselling, screwing and bodging. His eyes will shine as he shows you his range of power tools and grades of sandpaper. Not for him the current fashion for inviting TV crews to come into your home to complete a painless and highly public makeover. Indeed, the only real threat to his world is the disturbing modern trend for the lady of the house to get involved, and with it the discovery that most jobs might easily be completed in half the time.

Expressions to learn
Don't worry, I can knock this up myself in an afternoon.
Excuse me, have you got a number 5, tungsten-tipped, hydraulic bradawl shield?

Avoid saying
I'm not climbing that ladder - I might get dizzy!
Now, what was the phone number of that joiner chappie?

Oh, and when you've got a minute, the shower rail you put up in the bathroom yesterday has just fallen down.

31 *Ta-ta For Now*

In Britain, why does so long take *so long*? For the True Brit, parting is every bit as complicated and fraught with risk as greeting. We find it difficult to say Hello, and we find it hard to say Good-bye. And the bit in the middle is none too easy, either. We have to decide whether to kiss, shake hands, or execute one of those stiff, short-armed waves that we use to fend off unwelcome intimacies. We need time to select from an extensive repertoire of leave-taking expressions from *Well, I'll be on my way then* to a final faint *Cheers!* before disappearing over the brow of the hill.

Above all, we must try to avoid the awkwardness that can occur in extricating ourselves from a social encounter. One way is to order a taxi in advance: in the moments of flustered haste after the doorbell rings, the normal rules of leave-taking are waived and the long farewell amputated to a breathless, *Oh dear! Well! Thanks a lot! Bye!*

Expressions to learn
My goodness! Is that the time? We really must start thinking about making a move.
Don't do anything I wouldn't do!

Avoid saying
Are you still here?
Close the door on your way out.

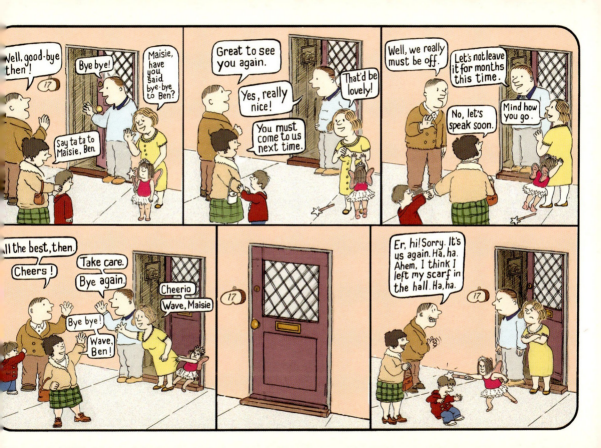

32 *The Future*

The pace of change is so very fast now, and globalised commercial culture so pervasive, does it still make any sense to talk of a 'national character'? Could it be the British are losing their traditional virtues of modesty, inhibition, irreverence, reserve, tolerance, irony, fair play, nostalgia and eager inebriation?

The white cliffs of Dover (which look distinctly grey from the ferryboat) are crumbling into the sea, and intensive farming methods have done for the bluebirds.

But something is sure to survive. I mean, there'll always be fish and chips on the menu - well, as long as there are a few cod left in the North Sea. And there'll always be a Royal Family, won't there? Well, at least until the popular press decide otherwise.

And when the independent British space programme has got underway at last, no doubt our True Brits will be there: planting runner beans in the Martian desert or complaining about the dust storms on Mercury. And, as the sun goes down through a sulphurous haze, and they settle down for the six-year long Jupiter winter, a steady ammoniac drizzle trickling down the window panes, he will look at her and she will look at him and, at precisely the same moment, both of them will say, "Now let's have a nice cup of tea!"